MISSISSIPPI STERNWHEELERS

MISSISSIPPI STERNWHEELERS

Pam and Gerry Zeck

illustrations by George Overlie

 Carolrhoda Books, Inc., Minneapolis

The authors wish to thank James S. Kosmo, President of the *Padelford Packet Boat Company* at Harriet Island in St. Paul, Minnesota, and the captains and crews of the sternwheelers *Jonathan Padelford* and *Josiah Snelling,* for their kind and enthusiastic cooperation. Special thanks are due to Captain William D. Bowell, Captain and Master of all vessels, for bringing sternwheelers back to the upper Mississippi River.

The photograph of the sidewheel paddle boat is used courtesy of the Minnesota Historical Society.

LIBRARY OF CONGRESS CATALOGING IN PUBLICATION DATA

Zeck, Pam.
Mississippi sternwheelers.

SUMMARY: Photographs and text describe the origins of sternwheel paddle boats and how they aided in the settling of the interior of the United States. Also included is a look at today's sternwheelers.

1. Mississippi River — Navigation — History — Juvenile literature. 2. Paddle steamers — History — Juvenile literature. I. Zeck, Gerry. II. Title.

HE630.M6Z42   386′.22436′0977   81-15553
ISBN 0-87614-180-7   AACR2

To the memory of our great grandparents,
John and Mary, who arrived in this country
by steaming up the Mississippi River aboard
a sternwheel paddle boat.

Two hundred years ago, the Mississippi was a wild and dangerous river. Uprooted trees were buried in the river's bottom. Their roots and branches stuck up into the water like spears. These "snags" could easily rip a hole in a birch-bark canoe or upset a trader's raft.

Floods, droughts, and log jams changed the river from week to week. Deep spots could suddenly become shallow. Overnight a whole section of the river could change its path. Traders traveling down the Mississippi had to learn a new river every time they made the trip. They never knew what to expect.

And then there were the currents! Traveling upstream was next to impossible. In the days before the steamboat was invented, the Mississippi was a one-way river. Traders floated their log rafts loaded with furs, bear oil, and honey downriver to St. Louis and New Orleans. Then they unloaded their goods, took their rafts apart, and sold the logs as lumber. They couldn't ship supplies back upriver because the currents were too fast for hand-powered boats. So frontiersmen had to rely on slow-moving horses and wagons instead.

Then, in 1807, Robert Fulton put a steam engine aboard his boat, the *Clermont*. The engine turned two huge paddle wheels—one on each side of the boat—that moved the *Clermont* through the waters of the Hudson River in New York. On its first trip, it went from New York City to Albany, a distance of 150 miles, in 32 hours—twice as fast as a wagon train.

But the *Clermont* and other early steamboats were designed for eastern rivers like the Hudson. These boats had deep, V-shaped bottoms (or hulls), and a paddle wheel on each side. They were called SIDEWHEELERS. Sidewheelers were great for steaming through deep water. But their bottoms were too deep for the shallow water of the upper Mississippi. And the paddle wheels always seemed to get smashed by snags in the Mississippi River.

In order to navigate the Mississippi, sidewheelers had to be redesigned. Their deep, V-shaped hulls were flattened so that they wouldn't get stuck on the Mississippi's sand bars. And their two side wheels became one wheel at the back (or stern), where it would be protected from snags by the hull. The new steamboats were called STERNWHEELERS.

Sternwheelers operated fairly simply. The stern wheel was connected to the steam engine inside the boat by a long piston rod, shown in the photograph on the left. The piston was attached to an arm that would turn the wheel. When the piston pushed the arm up, over, and around the hub (or clockwise in the photograph), the stern wheel pulled the boat backward through the water. When the engine was reversed, the piston pushed the arm counterclockwise and the stern wheel pushed the boat forward.

The boat was steered by rudders, called monkey rudders because they copied each other ("monkey see, monkey do"). Two rudders were located in front of the wheel, and two more behind it. When the captain turned the pilot wheel at the front of the boat, the rudders turned to steer the boat to the port (left) or to the starboard (right).

Sternwheelers arrived on the Mississippi River just in time to help American settlers develop the great interior of our country. The Mississippi River was the main highway into the new Minnesota Territories and beyond. The busiest years on the upper Mississippi were between 1849 and 1862. Crowded paddle boats steamed up and down the river every day. They carried almost half a million immigrants from the mouth of the Mississippi River at New Orleans all the way to St. Paul at the end of the navigable river. The paddle boats also carried supplies of cloth, furniture, tools, gun powder, and animals to the frontier. Paddle boats returning downstream carried grain and animal furs.

The arrival of a steamboat was always an important event during the early years of the frontier. Settlers who lived along the river could even tell the name of the steamboat by the sound of its whistle. The most exciting whistles belonged to the showboats. Showboats brought live entertainment to the frontier in the form of minstrel shows, dramatic theater, music, and dancing.

There were few wharfs, or docks, along the Mississippi River before dams were built to control the water level. But the landing platform at the front (or bow) of the sternwheeler could turn any river bank into a landing spot. The flat-bottomed boat gently bumped into the shoreline, the boat was secured by a line tied to a tree, and the landing platform was lowered to the ground.

But travel on the river was still dangerous. Steamboat captains steered their boats from the pilot house atop the highest deck, where they could see the river far ahead. But a captain needed help from his crew to steer through shallow water. A crew member at the bow of the boat would drop a pole or a weighted and knotted rope into the river to measure the depth of the water. This was called making a sounding. When the crew member yelled, "Mark Twain!" to the captain, it meant that the river was two fathoms (12 feet) deep and the course was safe.

Steamboats had to land frequently so that wood could be cut and hauled aboard for fuel. In the old days, flared crowns were put on top of the twin smokestacks. These crowns directed the heavy black smoke and hot sparks away from the boat and its precious cargo.

Few of the old wooden steamboats lasted more than five years on the river. When dirty steam engines were over-heated, the boilers exploded. The boats usually caught fire and then sank.

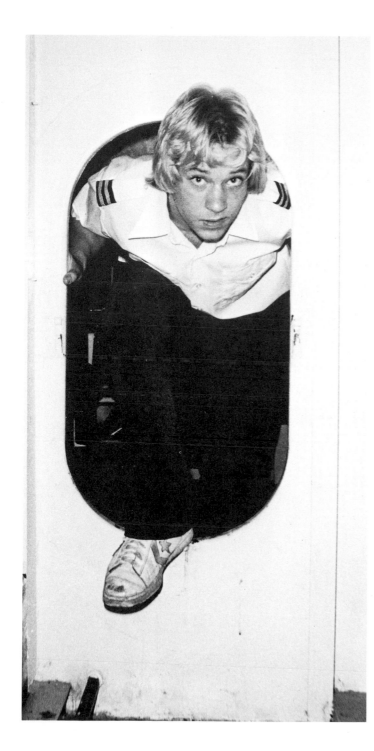

Modern sternwheelers are run by safe diesel engines that do not make black smoke or sparks. Diesel engines are smaller and more efficient than the old steam engines, too.

In order to inspect the engine compartment, which is located below the first deck, this crew member must pass through small doors called hatchways.

Fuel and water for drinking, cooking, and toilets are loaded into today's sternwheelers through "fill pipes" located near the bow of the boat.

But in most respects, the sternwheeler today still operates the way it used to in the old days. Crew members must regularly inspect the paddle wheel and grease all the moving parts to make sure the wheel turns smoothly.

There are fewer than two dozen official sternwheelers in the United States today. A few are registered as private yachts, at least two still ferry cars back and forth across the river, and some carry on the tradition of old showboats. But most sternwheelers today are short-distance passenger boats like the *Jonathan Padelford* in St. Paul, Minnesota. Every summer, the *Jonathan Padelford* and her sister ship, the *Josiah Snelling*, carry thousands of people on short trips up and down the Mississippi. After all passengers have boarded, the captain welcomes them over the boat's modern intercom.

Then three loud blasts from the steam whistle signal the boat's departure.

The old steamboats had from one to three decks for passengers and cargo. The fancier steamboats had cabins on one or more decks. The best sleeping cabins were on the highest deck, far away from the noisy steam engines. These boats also had a large public room, called the salon, where people gathered to talk, read, or dance. But ordinary steamboats had few luxuries, and on many of them the passengers had to share space with bulky cargo and even animals.

The *Jonathan Padelford* has two passenger decks. On the main deck the salon is decorated with brass lanterns and paintings of the old river heroes. The second deck has a large open space which is ideal for dancing or just sitting on benches and watching the river scenery.

The Mississippi River is a water highway for many industries. Small but powerful towboats like the *Sophie Rose* (above right) are the work horses of the river. The most powerful towboats can push as many as thirty fully-loaded barges at once.

Great rafts of steel barges bring coal and fuel oil up the river where it is needed to heat homes and schools and factories. Grain, which is brought from the Great Plains by railroad, is stored in giant grain elevators next to the river, then loaded into covered steel barges (lower right) and towed down river to feed lots and flour mills and bakeries.

Following the American Civil War, many railroads were built to cross the Great Plains. The railroads hauled freight and passengers to the western frontier and grain back to the eastern United States. Soon railroads replaced rivers as the most important highways into the new frontier.

This rare railroad swing bridge was built in 1915 by the Chicago, Milwaukee and St. Paul Railway. It pivots on a large concrete piling sunk deeply into the river bed. When a large boat approaches the bridge, the captain signals the bridgemaster. If there is no train coming, the bridgemaster opens the bridge so that the boat can pass through.

The captains of the *Jonathan Padelford* and *Josiah Snelling* exchange pleasant greetings over the marine radio. In the old days the meeting of steamboats wasn't always so friendly. Competition between rival steamboat captains was great. Each captain wanted to deliver more cargo and passengers faster than the others. Steamboat races, like the famous series of races between the *Natchez* and the *Robert E. Lee*, often risked the safety of passengers and crew when the steam engines were pushed to their limits. Boiler explosions and boat sinkings were so common that sunken hulls made parts of some rivers almost impassable.

The first sternwheelers on the upper Mississippi couldn't navigate beyond Fort Snelling where the Mississippi meets the Minnesota River. The river was too shallow and rocky north of the Fort. But then, in the early 1900s, the U.S. Army Corps of Engineers built Lock and Dam Number One. The new dam raised the water level by holding back the water upstream. It made the river navigable up to the flour mills of Minneapolis. The lock, a huge channel through the dam, allowed large boats to get from one side of the dam to the other.

Every lock has two gates: an upstream gate and a downstream gate. At least one gate is always closed.

When the downstream gate is open, a boat traveling upstream can enter the lock. Once the boat is inside the lock, the lockmaster closes the gate. Then he opens a valve in the floor of the lock and the lock fills with water from upstream. When the lock is full of water, the boat is at the same level as the upstream water. Then the lockmaster opens the upstream gate and the boat is free to leave.

When the upstream gate is open, a boat traveling down river can enter the lock. After the gate is closed, the water level is lowered through valves in the floor of the lock. When the boat is at the same level as the downstream water, the downstream gate is opened and the boat moves on.

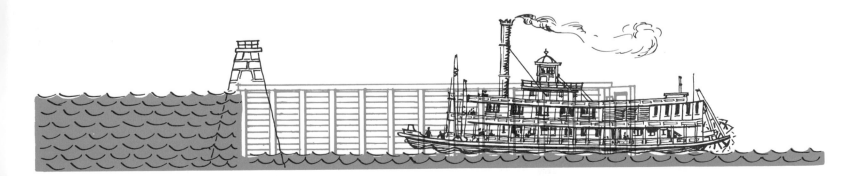

The *Jonathan Padelford* enters Lock and Dam Number One through the downstream gate. *Jonathan* is headed upstream.

The upstream water is held back by a steel gate. As boats enter the lock, the lock-master drops long safety lines and the boats are secured to the wall.

Hydraulic valves fill the lock with six million gallons of upstream water in less than eight minutes. When the water level in the lock is the same as the water level above the lock, the lockmaster opens the gate and the boats are free to leave.

The Mississippi River, also known as "The Father of the Waters," has changed a lot during the last hundred years. Many of the problems faced by the riverboat pilots of the 1800s no longer exist today. But it is still possible to travel the Mississippi on replicas of the original sternwheel paddle boats that brought so many people and so much change to America.